S.A-N.T.A. C.L.A.U.S

ALAN PARR

A mathematical adventure for KS2

IMAGINATIVE MINDS   Imaginative Minds Ltd © 2008

Published by
Imaginative Minds Ltd © 2008

ISBN 978-1-904806-28-8

Edited by Brian Asbury
Design & production by Al Stewart
Illustration by Pat Murray

IM
IMAGINATIVE
MINDS

Introduction

S.A-N.T.A. C.L.A.U.S. is a mathematical adventure game suitable for various ages, but particularly those working in Key Stage 2 of the National Curriculum. Over the last few years, I've put a lot of effort into developing such mathematical adventure games. They have many advantageous features, which can be summarised into two main areas:

- *they are tremendously enjoyable for children, who work with real excitement and consequently with a concentration and commitment which are often far beyond their normal levels (this tends to be very noticeable with low achievers)*

- *they are easy for teachers to administer, offering them the chance to observe the ways their children go about the process of solving problems.*

A further advantage is that such adventures meet all the specifications of OFSTED and the like – even that daunting section of non-statutory guidance which mentions words like 'fascination', 'motivation', 'pleasure', and 'enjoyment'.

What is an adventure game?

A mathematical adventure game has many of the desirable features of computer-based adventures. Most notable is the fact that all the activities are linked by a common theme and an overall problem which the children are trying to solve – perhaps they're trying to escape from a giant's castle, or explore a desert island.

However, they have a number of advantages over computer adventure games. To start with, there's the obvious fact that no computer is necessary, nor any other special equipment apart from that which is normally to be found in any classroom. Also, unlike most computer-based adventures, the tasks here can be attempted in any order, so no-one needs get stuck at any point in the game simply because there's one problem they haven't yet been able to solve. Neither is any special expertise needed from the teacher – indeed, it is often a good idea to invite a parent or other adult to do the actual administration, so that the teacher can concentrate entirely upon observing just how the children go about tackling problems.

Typically, one of my adventures will have eight or nine problems for the children, working in pairs, to solve. Each problem has a range of possible answers, and each

answer will give the children a piece of information so that, when they've solved all the problems, they'll have the data they need to solve one final problem. The snippets of information can be obtained in any order, and there's no need (unless you wish) for each one to be checked before they move on to finding the next – hence the ease of administration. But of course, correct information comes only from correct answers, so, if they have any wrong answers at all, children will not be able to solve the overall problem. The need to be 100% correct serves only to increase their motivation; contrast this with a more traditional lesson, where 80% success rate may be seen as a good performance.

Usually, my target time for completing the whole adventure is about 1½-2 hours, but children will usually be happy to work for considerably longer if necessary. Whenever possible, I like to include extension ideas for follow-up work, both in mathematics and in other subjects as well.

Surely there must be some disadvantages to these wonderful experiences? Well, they can take a lot of thinking up, but that's really the author's problem rather than yours. There is also a certain amount of photocopying and other preparation to do, but this should take no more than an hour or so, and most can be done by a parent helper (see the notes on 'Preparation' on page 5 for details).

Some of this probably sounds hugely mystifying so far but, in practice, teachers and pupils whom I have never met assure me that the adventures are easy to use and that they do meet all the aims I try to build in. For example, when 'S.A.-N.T.A. C.L.A.U.S.' originally appeared in *Strategies* magazine's Christmas 1995 edition (Vol. 6 no. 1), among the comments it attracted were the following:

- ❖ *'No special equipment was needed, the instructions were clear and my preparation was minimal.'*

- ❖ *'Thank you! It was fascinating to see the different approaches to the problems.'*

- ❖ *'The children enjoyed it immensely, becoming more and more engrossed as they tackled each activity. They begged me to "Make up another one, Miss".'*

Teachers' notes

To introduce this special Christmas adventure, show the children the introductory sheet on page 14 and tell them that they have been invited to apply for a job helping a supplier of Christmas gifts. Whether you want to draw the significance of the company's initials (S.A-N.T.A. C.L.A.U.S.) to their attention is left to your own discretion. The sheet tells them that they will be tried out in several of the company's departments, each of which will give them a problem to solve. After they have read the introductory sheet, divide them into pairs and hand out copies of the first problem ('The Main Office', which you will find on page 15).

Each pair will also need a copy of the answer sheets (pages 25-26), to make notes on and record their answers. Each problem has several possible answers, but only one is correct. So, if they think the answer to the 'Main Office' problem is 84, they need to make a note of the word PRESENT, but they think the answer is 93 then they need to record BIRTH.

Including this initial task (and you may want to check they are familiar with the term 'digit' before they begin), there are nine tasks in all, so they will collect nine words in the course of the session. It is worth emphasising that all the words are different, and that a single wrong word mean that they will be unable to complete their final problem, in which case they won't get their Christmas job after all (incidentally, by the time they've done all nine tasks, they should have a pretty good idea of just who their employer might be!).

The final task, which I prefer to introduce late in the session, can be found on page 12.

The steps involved in the administration procedure are summarised on page 6.

Additional points

There are bound to be some children who are weaker readers but, as far as possible, any help should be restricted to the reading itself. One of the principal purposes of any adventure is to put every child into the position of having to solve problems, and the motivation provided by the circumstances and the overall theme is normally sufficient to make children show levels of commitment and attainment which are well beyond their normal standards of performance. In my trials,

teachers commented several times on the quality of the work of those who normally find maths a chore.

Remember, though, that achievement in National Curriculum Attainment Target 1 ('Using and applying mathematics') can only be shown if children are making choices and decisions for themselves. If you make use of classroom helpers, warn them against giving 'helpful' guidance too early. What seems an obvious method to adults may be neither obvious nor helpful to children.

I've carefully avoided any mention of a target age group. When I began devising S.A-N.T.A. C.L.A.U.S. I really had Years 5 to 6 children in mind. However, as things developed, the nature of the target group began to be more diffuse. Many of the activities may be equally well offered to rather younger children, so one way of using the adventure would be to allow Year 6 children to do it first, and then subsequently to allow each of them to take responsibility for a pair of Year 3/4 children as the younger ones try it themselves.

Some of the most sympathetic teaching I've ever seen came about when a Year 5 class took the problems of an adventure and adapted them for children throughout their JMI school. They introduced the activities in a dramatised version of the adventure, and groups worked with each class throughout the morning. Some children who attended the 9.30am assembly were still engrossed in solving the adventure when their parents came to collect them at the end of the afternoon!

Preparation for the adventure

1) Photocopy each of the nine task sheets on pages 15 to 23. Sheets 2 to 9 don't get written on or used up, so it's not necessary to have any more than two or three copies of each at most. Cheap Nyrex wallets (about 4p each from stationers) will protect them and make storage easier if you want to begin your preparation for next Christmas early! However, each child (or at least each pair) will need a copy of the first problem ('The Main Office', page 15).

2) Photocopy the introductory sheet (page 14). Again, each child or pair will need a copy of this page.

3) Photocopy the two answer sheets (pages 25 to 26). Each pair will need both sheets for recording their progress. If it's convenient, the answer sheets can be put back to back on a single sheet.

4) Photocopy page 24, which duplicates the patterns shown on task sheet 9 ('The Decorations Area'). This is not essential, but it is helpful if each pair can be given a copy of this when they tackle task sheet 9, so that the children can cut it up and manipulate the separate items for themselves.

5) Photocopy the final certificates from page 27 (one per child). I prefer to keep these out of sight until the end of the adventure.

6) There's no need to make special arrangements for any equipment; none of the activities should need anything that's not part of a normal classroom.

Administration

1) Tell the children they have been invited to apply for a Christmas job, helping organise deliveries of Christmas cards and presents. They've got an introductory task to do, which will be followed by eight more. Give them the introductory sheet (page 14) and the 'Main Office' problem (page 15).

2) All nine tasks are on separate sheets, none of which should be written on. All working out can be done on the answer sheets, so each pair needs a copy of the two answer sheets (pages 25-26).

3) The tasks can be done in any order.

4) For each task, children work in their pairs and can use whatever apparatus or (legal) methods they wish.

5) Every activity has several possible answers; when they've decided on the answer, children should refer to their answer sheet and look up the word corresponding to that answer. So if they are doing the first task ('The Main Office') and think the answer is 84, then the word they need is PRESENT.

6) When they have done every activity, they'll have nine words. They will then be given one final task to solve (see page 12).

7) And lastly, when they have solved the final task, they can be presented with their Certificate of Achievement (page 27). A nice additional activity can be to put the copies of the certificate in a folder and to hide this somewhere in the classroom. Children love searching for the folder and enjoy hiding it somewhere fresh for discovery by the next group to finish.

Answers and extensions to the activities

Task 1 – The Main Office

The answer, and the only number which meets all five criteria, is 57, so the children should note the word **STABLE**. At this stage, they have no knowledge of why they're collecting words, which is all part of the fun. They may notice that all the words they collect have some connection with Christmas (but then, so have all the ones they reject!).

As OFSTED's report *The Teaching and Learning of Number in Primary Schools* pointed out, children enjoy puzzling out questions like this, and also composing them for themselves. Kirsty, reputedly a less able Year 3 girl, offered:

- ❖ *'It's got two digits.'*
- ❖ *'It's in the five times table.'*
- ❖ *'Both digits are the same.'*

She also supplied further clues for those who needed them:

- ❖ *'It's higher than 50.'*
- ❖ *'It's between 50 and 60.'*

Task 2 – The Dining Room

There are actually 16 different menus possible, so the coded answer is **GOLD**. Initial estimates may be nowhere near 16 and, to be able to answer the question, children need to find all the possibilities. Although the first few possibilities may be identified fairly randomly, finding them all is likely to require some organised searching. It is well worth watching and listening:

- ❖ *Do children call upon counters or other apparatus?*
- ❖ *How do they keep check of possibilities and make sure there are no duplications?*
- ❖ *How can they convince themselves – and others – that they've found all the possibilities?*

Questions such as 'how many ways/combinations are there?' are classic starting points for investigations. The idea for this one was conceived when I noticed my local Tesco store was offering a breakfast menu where you are allowed to choose four items from six (bacon, baked beans, tomatoes, scrambled egg, hash browns and mushrooms).

Task 3 – The Christmas Card Shop

A total of 20 cards will be sent altogether, and the total cost will be £7.00, so the word to find is **NATIVITY**. Once again, however, there are many possible ways for children to approach this problem, from the very concrete to the wholly abstract. How do they handle the money part of the calculation? As an extended addition, or multiplication? Mentally, on paper, or with a calculator?

A similar question is the very productive 'handshakes' investigation – if everybody in the room shakes hands with everybody else, how may handshakes are needed? Easy enough to find this with a group of five, but a bit harder when you have 30+ in your class! One of the nice things about the handshake problem is that, as the numbers increase, you're almost forced to move from a concrete approach to a more abstract one, quite likely passing through a diagrammatic method on the way. A suitably Christmassy implementation would be to ask how many Christmas crackers would be needed if everyone in the class were able to pull a cracker with everyone else.

Task 4 – The Loading Warehouse

Sleigh D is the only one which will hold all the parcels, so the word to look for is TREE. This question is, of course, to do with capacity and volume, but it is offered in a form which doesn't immediately invite a knee-jerk response of 'length times breadth times height'. Expect many children, even Year 6 ones who have done work on volumes of cuboids, to call upon cubes to solve it – and expect some younger children to be able to solve the question in their heads!

A very tempting follow-up would be to ask children to devise nets to construct the various sleighs:

- *Do they all need the same amount of card?*
- *What possible sleighs are there for a specific number of cubes?*
- *Which ones uses least/most card?*
- *Which would actually make the best sleigh?*

Task 5 – The Purchasing Department

A natural strategy that children sometimes use to tackle certain questions is to look at the answers and work backwards. By and large I don't object to this, since there are many occasions when we're happy to encourage such an approach in mathematics (isn't finding the difference between two numbers by counting on or back an example of this?). I do have to be careful, however, that this approach isn't too rewarding, and there are occasions when I make sure the possible answers are not too revealing. Therefore, in this case, none of the indicated sets is correct. The only set of three items adding up to £3.00 consists of the jelly mouse (15p), the joke book (95p) and the face paints (£1.90), so the '?' answer is the right one, and the required word is **GIFT**.

There are a lot of possible sets of three items (finding the exact number – 20 – is another investigation in its own right), so finding the solution by trial and error would be a laborious process. However, short cuts are possible, so eavesdropping might tell you if the children notice that felt pens (79p) are a red herring because they are the only item whose price doesn't have 5 or 0 in the units digit. The Christmas annual is another item that can be ignored, since it would leave only 50p for buying the other two items.

Task 6 – The Stables

Mac is in stall 3, so the word **INN** is correct.

Being able to interpret and use mathematical language, both written and spoken, is an important skill and is one of the core strands of 'Using and applying mathematics'. From the many KS2 SATs papers that I have marked it has been very apparent that

far too many children haven't developed these skills. In order to remedy this, a child's mathematical diet should regularly include activities like:

❖ *Can you describe a square without using your hands?*

❖ *How would you sort these shapes/toys/fruits/...?*

❖ *What have these items got in common?*

❖ *How are they different?*

Task 7 – The Map Centre

The two correct routes are 1 and 3, so the word is **EXCITEMENT**.

In my experience, most children enjoy tackling questions like these, but all too often even the older pupils are not very good at them. It's useful to have a little model person to walk through the routes, or even chalk the road network on the playground so the children can give and follow the actual instructions. Of course, there's no better way to master the giving of instructions of direction and movement than by using a programmable toy, or Logo.

Task 8 – The Scheduling Section

A correct route needs:

❖ *to start and finish at the Headquarters*

❖ *to visit each of the three towns.*

It does not need to traverse every section of road and, indeed, the best route will avoid unnecessary sections. A suitable route would be HQ – Midton – Lexford – HQ – Ketby – HQ. This is 69km, so the appropriate word is **REINDEER**.

The activity has two particular aspects to interest the teacher. The first is how the children go about finding the best route – whether they use trial and error, or trial and improvement, and how they decide that particular sections of the network are uneconomic. The second aspect is, of course, the arithmetical side; to find the answer, they will have to add several two digit numbers. How many children do this by:

❖ *writing them down and adding them in the conventional vertical sum? (My guess is precious few!)*

❖ *using a calculator?*

❖ *using a mental method?*

And what is the range of the different methods called upon by the class as a whole?

In common with some of the other questions, this one went through several versions. One involved four towns rather than three, and one involved different starting and finishing places. I also rather hankered for a problem which involved times and perhaps the reading of timetables, so another version involved asking how long the whole trip would take when you allow for loading times, travel time at, say, 2 minutes per kilometre and 45 minutes at each town to make the deliveries.

Task 9 – The Decorations Area

The outline shapes of the 15 baubles are equilateral triangles, squares, regular pentagons, regular hexagons, and the internal shapes are the same, but smaller. The picture shows all possible combinations except one (external hexagon, internal pentagon), so the required word is **EVENING**.

One aspect of this problem is concerned with observing and classifying, and another is about shapes and their names and properties. A surprisingly large number of children are able to recognise triangles and squares on sight, but feel than pentagons and hexagons are slightly different versions of the same thing.

This task is made more accessible if a copy of page 24, which duplicates the shapes on the problem sheet, is given to each pair to allow children to cut out the fifteen shapes and sort them physically.

Of course, asking children to design their own complete sets of baubles makes an excellent follow-up.

The final task to be completed can be found on the next page. On the page following that, you will find some advice as offered by my 'guinea-pigs' who tested the adventure.

The final task

(BE SURE TO KEEP THIS PAGE OUT OF SIGHT AT ALL TIMES)

Once the children have their nine words, you can tell them that, if they take the initial letters of their nine answers, they should be able to rearrange them to make a word connected with Christmas. Once they can convince you that they have discovered the word, they have completed the adventure and can receive their certificate of competence.

The nine words are:

STABLE (The Main Office)

GOLD (The Dining Room)

NATIVITY (The Christmas Card shop)

TREE (The Loading Warehouse)

GIFT (The Purchasing Department)

INN (The Stables)

EXCITEMENT (The Map Centre)

REINDEER (The Schedule Section)

EVENING (The Decoration Area)

Thus, the initial letters are SGNTGIERE, and the word they are looking for is **GREETINGS**. Nine correct answers are necessary; there is no combination involving any incorrect answer which can possibly lead to the right word.

Advice from testers

(courtesy of the children at Bishop Wood Junior and Grove Road Primary Schools: Laura, Laura, Victoria, Alex, Holly, Sarah, Joseph, Polly and others)

We think you shouldn't go too quickly, because you will make mistakes. Always take time on your investigations.

Read the instructions carefully, otherwise you will find the task hard.

Check your answers more than once because you may find you get a different answer. This is what happened to us!

Don't look at other people's answers, because mostly everyone at the start had them wrong!

Never get impatient with each other.

Don't bother asking Mr Parr for information because you're wasting your time. (I was very proud of this one – A.P.)

Whatever you do, don't give up, always keep going.

Are you good enough to work for our Christmas team?

Our famous company has more work than it can handle at this time of year, and so we need to employ extra Christmas help.

There are many vacancies in all nine departments – the buying section, the Christmas card shop, the delivery service, etc.

Come at once to the Headquarters of the:

Special All-Night Transport Agency
Collecting, Loading And Unloading Service

Can you convince us that you're the person we're looking for?

Apply at the MAIN OFFICE.

TASK SHEET 1

You'll need to find the...
Main Office.

Here are some clues to help you. The office:

* has a two-digit number,
* both digits are more than 4,
* the two digits add up to 12,
* both digits are odd,
* the units digit is more than the tens digit.

TASK SHEET 2

The Dining Room

At lunchtime, the kitchen staff prepare a meal for all the workers.

Every meal must have:

- one item from list A,
- one from list B,
- and one from list C.

Every meal is different, so no one has exactly the same meal as anyone else.

How many different meals are there?

A
SOUP
OR
FRUIT JUICE

B
TURKEY
OR GOOSE
OR SALMON
OR
VEGETARIAN

C
CHRISTMAS PUDDING
OR
MINCE PIES

TASK SHEET 3

The Christmas Card Shop

Five friends come into the shop. Each person in the shop is going to send a Christmas card to everyone else. All cards cost 35p each.

How much will they spend between them?

TASK SHEET 4

The Loading Warehouse

On the big night, you have a load of parcels to deliver. All the parcels are packed in identical cubic boxes. Your load has 38 parcels.

Which sleigh will you choose? There are five possible sleighs and you know their maximum loads:

- sleigh A takes a load 9 boxes long, 2 wide and 2 high
- sleigh B takes a load 4 boxes long, 4 wide and 2 high
- sleigh C takes a load 4 boxes long, 3 wide and 3 high
- sleigh D takes a load 5 boxes long, 4 wide and 2 high
- sleigh E takes a load 6 boxes long, 3 wide and 2 high

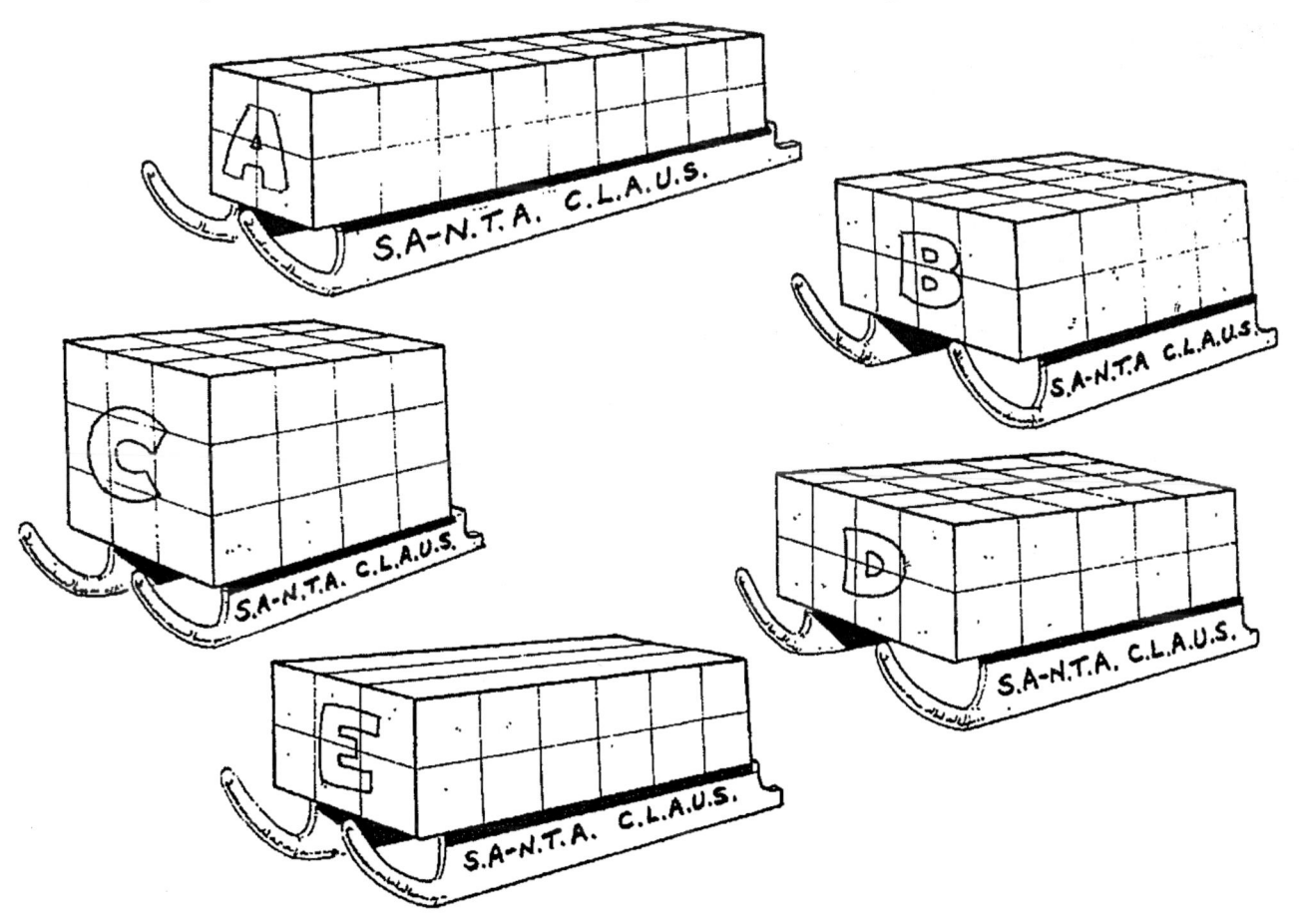

TASK SHEET 5

The Purchasing Department

Can you choose *three* different gifts to go in a Christmas stocking?

The total cost of the three items must be *exactly* £3.00.

- Christmas Annuals £2.50 each
- Joke Books 95p each
- Jelly Mouse 15p each
- Face Paints £1.90
- Felt Tip Pen Set 79p each
- Card Games 75p each

TASK SHEET 6

The Stables

You've been given your own reindeer to deliver the parcels. The reindeer is called Mac. Can you find which stall Mac is in?

- Rudolf is the one with the shiny nose
- Zigger is at one end
- Mac is next to Bluebell
- Skip is *not* next to Zigger
- Bluebell and Zigger are next to each other.

TASK SHEET 7

The Map Centre

You have to deliver some Christmas post to families who live in the High View block of flats.

The Centre computer gives you four routes for getting there – but only two are correct! Which routes will get you to the right place?

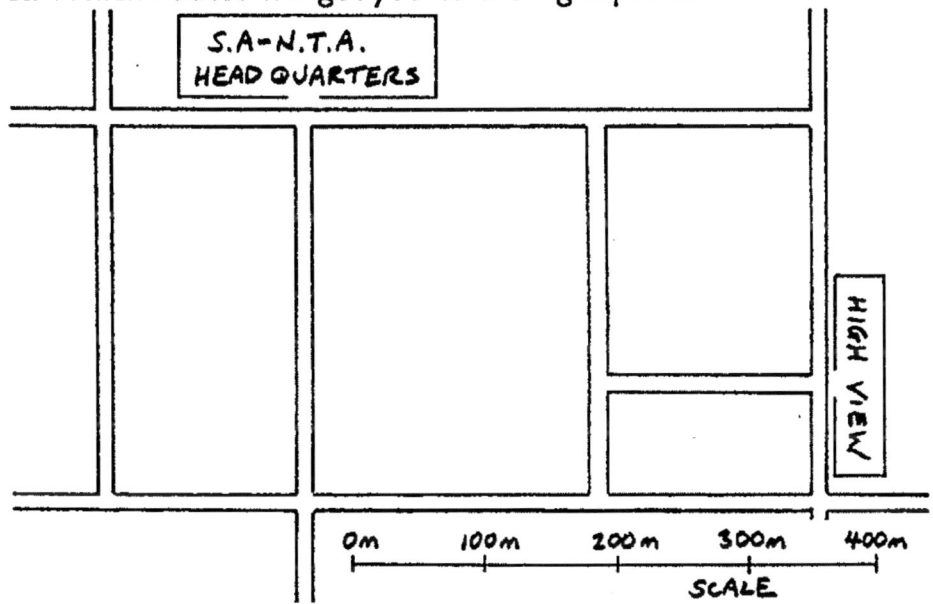

```
Route 1
 ↦  leave the headquarters building by the front entrance,
 ↦  turn left and walk to the end of the street,
 ↦  turn right,
 ↦  High View is the big building on your left.

Route 2
 ↦  leave the headquarters building by the front entrance,
 ↦  turn right,
 ↦  go as far as the crossroads,
 ↦  turn left,
 ↦  go to the end of the street,
 ↦  High View is the building facing you.

Route 3
 ↦  leave the headquarters building by the front entrance,
 ↦  turn left and walk about 400m down the road,
 ↦  turn right,
 ↦  the entrance to High View is about 200m down the road on your left.

Route 4
 ↦  leave the headquarters building by the front entrance,
 ↦  cross the road and go down the street facing you,
 ↦  turn left at the end,
 ↦  High View is about 200m down the road on your left.
```

TASK SHEET 8

The Scheduling Section

You have some parcels to take to the towns of Ketby, Lexford and Midton. Of course, you must start (and finish) at Headquarters.

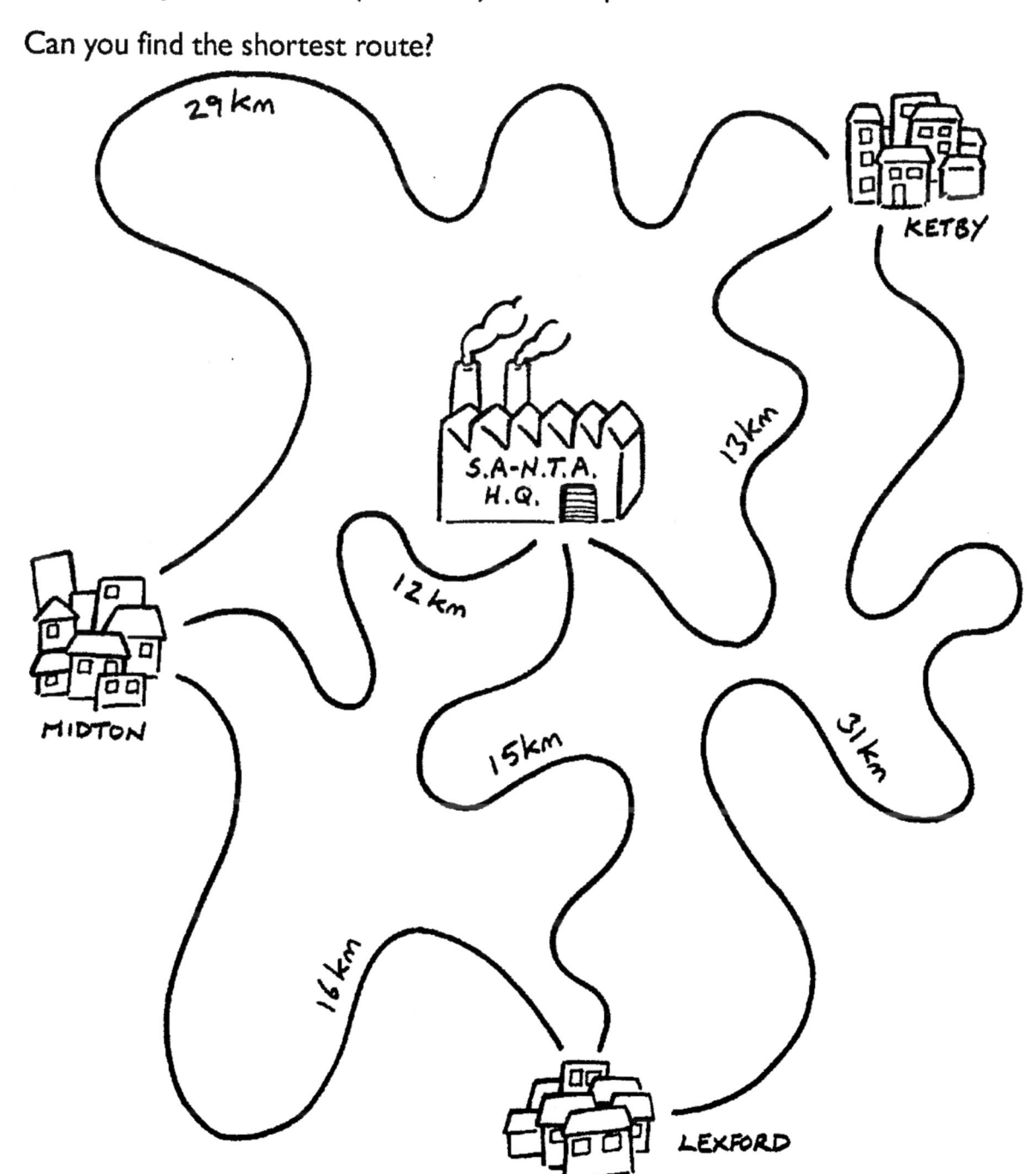

Can you find the shortest route?

Roads shown on map:
- HQ to Ketby (via northern route): 29 km
- HQ to Ketby (direct): 13 km
- HQ to Midton: 12 km
- HQ to Lexford: 15 km
- Ketby to Lexford: 31 km
- Midton to Lexford: 16 km

TASK SHEET 9

The Decorations Area

There should be 16 items in a set of Christmas decorations. All 16 are different.

One set has fallen on the floor and you can only find 15 of the items. What do you think the missing piece looks like?

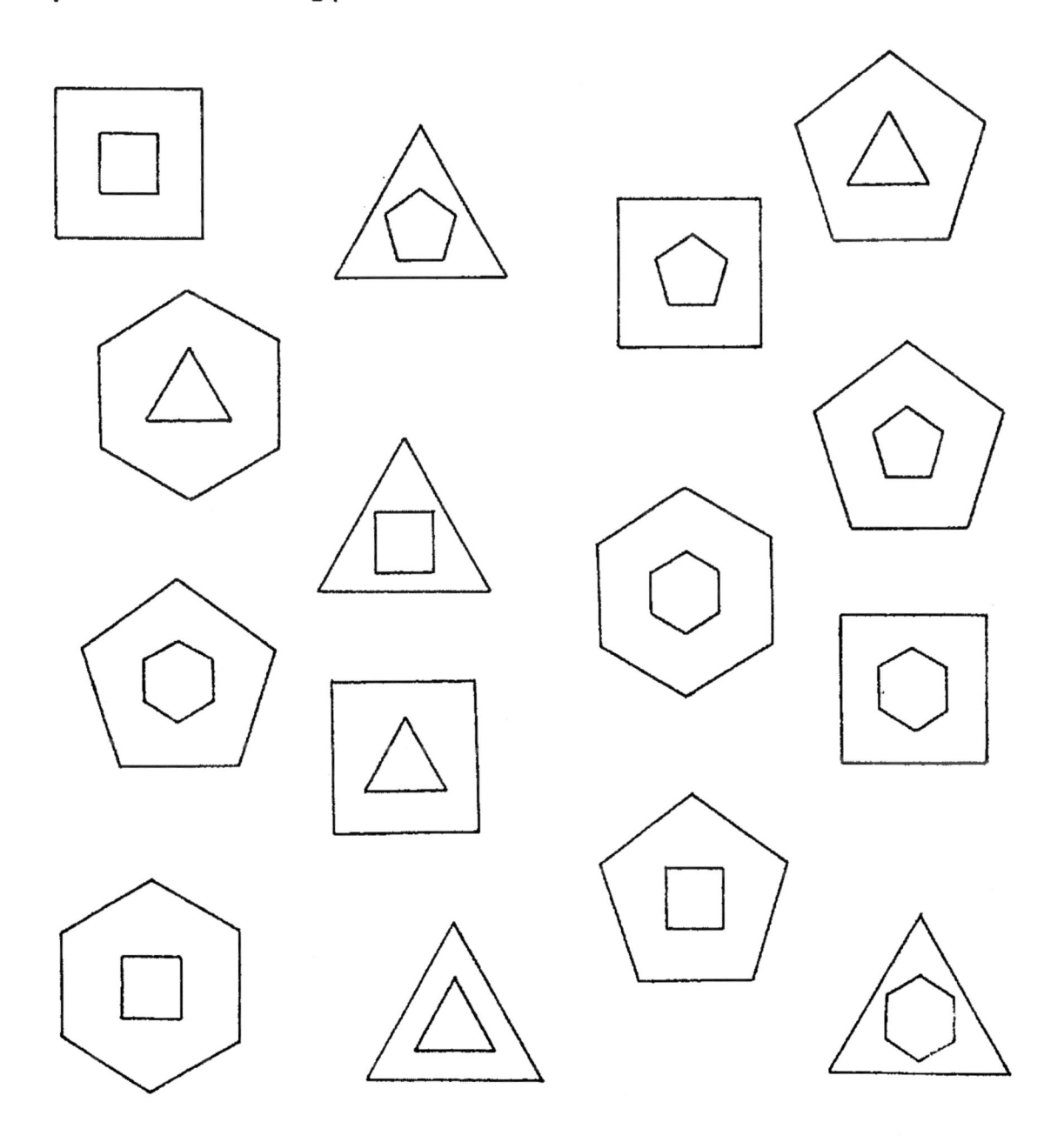

THE DECORATIONS AREA (Sheet 2)

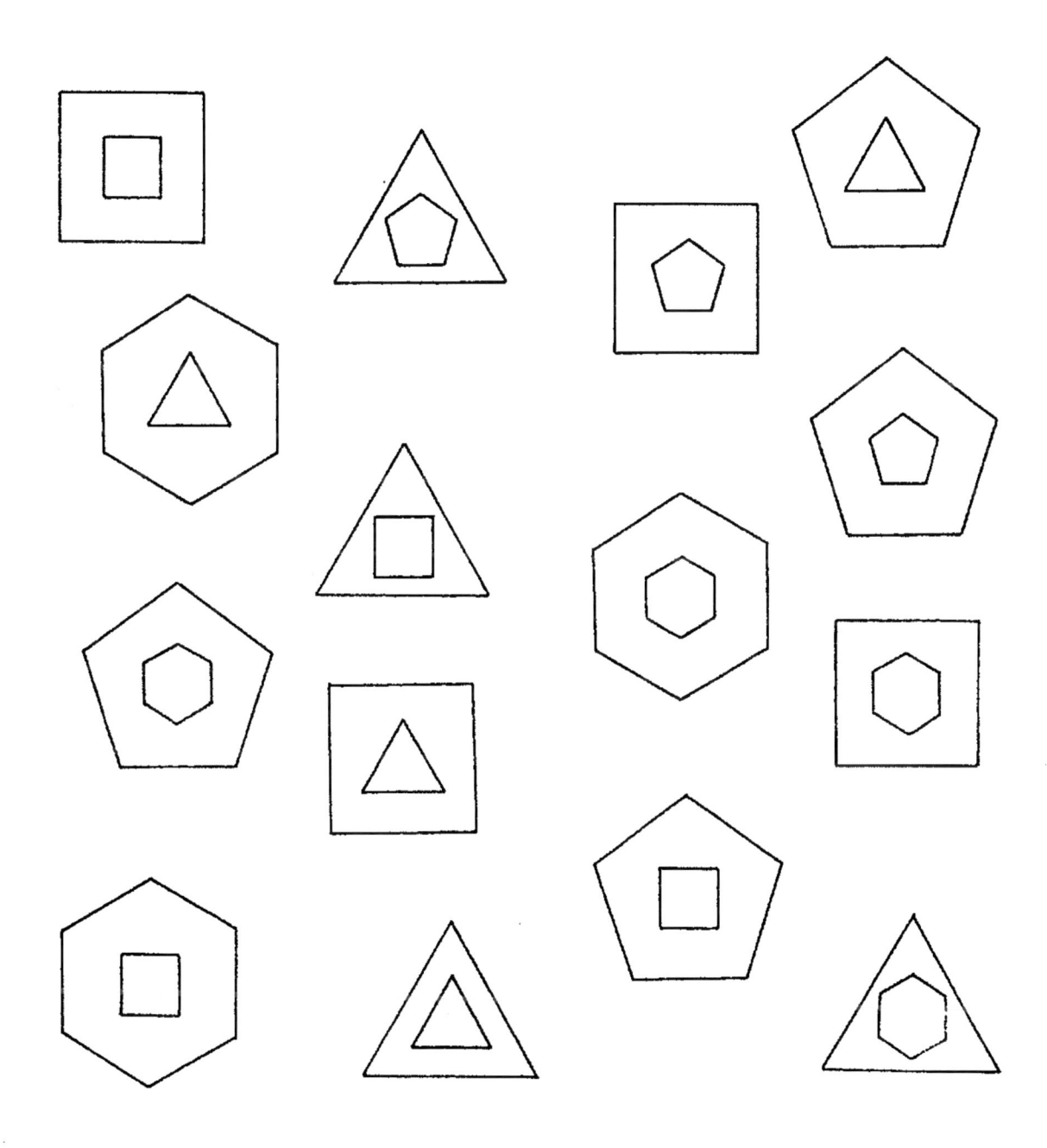

Answer sheet 1

The Main Office
The number of the office is:

84	PRESENT
57	STABLE
66	POSTMAN
75	CAROL
93	BIRTH

The Christmas Card Shop
Together they spend:

less than £2	MANGER
between £2 and £4	ANGELS
between £4 and £6	PUDDING
between £6 and £8	NATIVITY
more than £8	VISIT

The Dining Room
The number of different menus is:

fewer than 6	CAKE
between 6 and 9	HYMN
between 10 and 14	MISTLETOE
between 15 and 18	GOLD
more than 18	FIR-TREE

The Loading Warehouse
You need to choose:

sleigh A	HOLIDAY
sleigh B	JOSEPH
sleigh C	DECORATIONS
sleigh D	TREE
sleigh E	PARTY

The Purchasing Department
The three gifts are:

mouse, annual, face paints	MARY
game, felt pens, joke book	FIELDS
mouse, felt pens, face paints	CARD
annual, game, joke book	HOLLY
?, ?, ?	GIFT

Answer sheet 2

The Stables
Mac is in:

stall 1	PUDDING
stall 2	MYRRH
stall 3	INN
stall 4	CRACKERS
stall 5	YULETIDE

The Map Centre
The two correct routes are:

1 and 2	CANDLE
1 and 3	EXCITEMENT
1 and 4	MINCE PIE
2 and 3	FRANKINCENSE
2 and 4	HEROD
3 and 4	PAPER-CHAINS

The Decorations Area
The missing piece is:

(triangle)	WRAPPING-PAPER
(pentagon)	EVENING
(pentagon)	XMAS
(hexagon)	PANTOMIME

The Scheduling Section
The shortest route is:

less than 70km	REINDEER
between 70km and 74km	BETHLEHEM
between 75km and 79km	CHURCH
more than 79km	LIGHTS

Congratulations

on achieving the high standard required by every department of

S.A-N.T.A. C.L.A.U.S.

I recommend that

....

receives suitable reward on December 25th.

signed Santa Claus

(Founder and Managing Director)

About the author

Alan Parr is a primary mathematics consultant and lives in Tring, Hertfordshire. He is always delighted to hear from teachers and pupils who have used one of his adventures.

Acknowledgements

My very grateful thanks are due to numerous people who have helped in all sorts of ways, including everyone who responded so favourably to previous adventures, and especially the schools who tested *S.A-N.T.A. C.L.A.U.S.* – many thanks for all their help to the children and teachers of Bishop Wood Juniors and Grove Road Primary, Tring.